RIVERS & STREETS

poems by
GARY BECKER

Published by Gary Becker

ISBN - 1-59196-041-X

published by Gary Becker

printed in U.S. by Instantpublisher.com
on acid-free paper

cover art by Gary Becker
www.intres.com/garybecker

CONTENTS

FLOODED ROAD

RIVERS

THIRST

Turn on your faucet
fill a glass
with water's journey

a drop of ice
from mountain snow
drips
down into streams with granite jaws
flowing through pine coned cathedrals
over deep meadows
adorned with blossoms and bees
to hot flatland farms
sweetened with peaches and cream
between old pickup trucks
and frosty cones
through rows of corn
and crows on fence posts
by awning shaded fruit stands
around frog woven egg jewels
floating on ponds
with splintered oars drifting
on down through catfish bottomed sloughs
into dark murky pipes
deep tunnels and long tubes
out into daylight
through gleaming chrome sculpture

into
your sparkling awareness
and gratitude

MOTHER SEA

I went back home today
but I didn't go in.
I stood at the door
just listening to the waves
of memory crashing
the white foam of longing
onto the sand at my feet.
The soothing voice of deep water
sang its comforting frightening truth
no words could ever convey
from the never ending ritual of salt scripture
written in our blood
pounding like breakers on rock
in veins that pump
unending prayers to the sea
in the cathedral of the heart.
Every moment of my life
that I thought to impose my righteous will
puts on fresh robes of humility
and bows at the feet
of the Giver of all gifts.
Who taught me to be right?
Who made me be wrong?
What had I tried to accomplish
By hurting other seekers of love?
Love is not a word.
It is a wave
whose power can sculpt rocks of stubbornness
into shapes of surrender.
Let me open the door now
of my own prison
And release the humble servant
knocking from inside my heart
with desire to relieve suffering.
This ocean that is home

is a majestic drop
of the infinite sea of forgiveness
promised before time
and delivered with each breath
taken in with faith
and given out with generosity
like a surging tide of spirit.

ANCIENT DREAMS

Whales are circling your campfire
blowing smoke signals from sea
with their vaporous virtuous breath.
Night critters steal your cookies
in your sleep from the food stash.
Little feet and giant fins
following faithfully the commandments
given to them by the One
who gave you yours
long ago and just now.
Nut gnawing rascals
ocean gulping monsters
scolding fathers
comforting mothers
encouraging companions
still wandering your memories
in the secret solitude
created especially for you
to light the infinite deep darkness.
Your real friend
sings eternity's lullaby
forever in your lonely ears.
Sometimes at night
near your small fire
you can hear it
above the distant howls of wild creatures
calling their own friends,
calling to the same One as you.
The crackling flames of your dreams
warm your fears
and lull you into a peaceful sleep
by this campfire that is your soul.

LISTEN TO WATER

I rushed down from mountain snow fields
excited and anxious to show you
what I could do with nothing

You left me some plastic plates for a tip
and metal trinkets that choked my fish
and string that strangled my turtles

I passed through your body
on my way to becoming rain
washing the filth in your rooms
and watering your plants

You entertained yourself with the magic
dance of my evaporation
and ignored the withered Indian corn
asking only for a small drop
for its dry red sand

You didn't notice
Or seem to care
since you were angry at your companion
for heaping less than deep praise
for your small behaviors
while a walrus pup swam in your scum

That's just too bad
since you need more of what you don't need

Somewhere in that locked vault of guilt
is the deed to benevolence
and a glass of water
you will gladly share
in the desert of triviality you inhabit
all alone
surrounded by thirsty friends

WHAT THE RIVER THINKS
ABOUT YOU

through long wet lips of sand
a little river is sighing for you
then startled by gravel in its throat
it chatters with the wind
about a storm
high in the mountains

its nosey current
listens to green secrets
in sisterhoods of nest-sheltering reeds
whispered to mud wading moose
unaware of a caterpillar
worshipping with a sun beam
in a blackberry church

this compassionate creek
sings to its boulders
ringing enlightening gongs
of cold water bells
in a litany of sympathy
for your sorrow
and the good times
you left behind
snagged
on some sharp bend in your stream
where a tractor is rusting
in night frost
and dew in a morning mist

this brook of blue darkness
with syllables of moonlight
sparkling on a necklace of waves
is luring your heart
with an irresistible crystal of mercy in its voice

carving canyons of wisdom
through suffering souls
washing their garments of despair
while they sleep
in its rock bed
dreaming of the sea

a river understands
what you don't
concerning small things on the surface
and deeper more violent mysteries
that bears use on fish
for their cute cubs
to grow fat with an innocent appetite

this stream of consciousness knows
the song of the beginning
is repeated at the end
by an earthquake
and a butterfly
duet

it sees quiet evening light
slipped onto your dark fingers
like jewels
made of love
so you will never feel pain
without it

this gift of miraculous water
continuously arrives as it departs
going nowhere at all
forever a river of faith
staying right here
with you
its mystical movement
motionless
in a mantra

of clear
icy
nothing

that forms
into droplets of tears
on your cheek

HOW ANIMALS COME TO MEETINGS

when you ask about
my investments
an owl
flies through my retina
looking for a rat

and those forms that need filling out
get trampled in mud
by running wolves in my mouth

the signature
you want at the bottom
is signed by a lobster
waving its eyes
from its red ceramic suit
while it visits its cousin
a rock
who doesn't say much

the spines on the pine cones
poke holes in the fine print of contracts
alphabetized by aphids and zebras

an inventory of assets
crucial to projected profits
is updated on grape vines
by very busy bees

you advise
that would be a wise move
as you shuffle the relevant papers
but I can't hear
above thunder in the mountains
and the nibbling of seeds
in a jack rabbit den

nothing is more important
than getting these documents registered
to protect me from the insecurity
of these snakes gently squeezing
my fingers of old age
where they wrap themselves warmly
and stick out their tongues

may I borrow a pen
to write you a check for
how much was that
oh yes I remember
a whale two hippos an armadillo
and three ants

and now if you will excuse me
I am late for another meeting
so I will just grab my
night raiding band of raccoons
and be on my way

HIGHWAY HYMN

O Creator of my soul

Give me the humility
to get out of the way
of the fast ones.
Let me not judge
their need to arrive there first.

Grant me the wisdom
to refrain from rushing
the ones who go slowly
for they might be my mother
or elderly father.

Let me not seek revenge
against those asleep at the wheel
who ignore my existence.
Perhaps they drive
with a broken heart.

Let the self righteous voice
in my head remain silent
not rousing the rabble
in my vigilante mind
to punish the ones using cars
as weapons of aggression against me.
Remind me rather to shift
to a gear of compassionate awareness
that its power
pour a drop of oil
from a well of empathy
into fuel tanks filled with rage.

May I always remember
the destination is in my heart

and not down the highway.
May I travel a pavement of peace
to a back road of honorable mystery.

May I not expect gratitude
for yielding generosity
but give it freely
and anonymously
accepting the warmth inside
as the only reward.

May I keep my hostile finger
in its holster
or use it only with the other ones
to form a sign language
of brotherhood.

May I never be concerned
with a few moments of lost time
but savor the sweet drops
of eternity
on the tip of my tongue
whispering love songs to the Sun
and romantic mantras for the Moon.

Breathe a tail wind blessing
O God of the antelope
eagle and earthworm
for steel camel caravans
rocketing over paved trade routes
to one horse town
Wyatt Earp Meccas
in the wild west of fantasy
on the way out of maddening brick
labyrinths of science and chaos.

May my carburetor
inhale nothing but crystal mountain air

and my pistons pump without effort
in cylinders of humming bird wings.
May I get there swiftly
in a hot rod from hell
but may it take forever
in a jalopy
on a dirt road through heaven
As I drive
with You riding shotgun at dawn
down the trail into sunset
to the great unknown.

A BRIEF MOMENT OF GRATITUDE

This early dawn morning
with winter chill
and quiet trees
I thank you
O Creator of my self
for these eyeballs
that see
gulls circling
pine trees inland
for respite from their stormy
ocean prairie.

I thank you
for these ears
that hear
the crow in the canyon
opening its black beak
to speak
one deep squawk
of primal poetry.

And these hands
that hold a cup of coffee
my secret fire
in a world of icy emeralds.

I thank you
for these lips
that form the words
my heart desires
to thank you with.

This dawn
I recall
the One who wanted

to make me
so that I would remember
to be thankful
for that.

ZEN BEAGLISM

I am reading Ram Dass
about compassion
and nothingness
when my puppy prances up
with a chewed red slipper
in her teeth
looking at me expectantly.

"Are you going to be a Buddha
or just a little dog?"
I ask her.

she growls
and shakes the slipper
yanking it from my hand.

MYSTIC LULLABY

I am here
now
with happiness
because I know
you are with me always
O whisperer of my name.

Yesterday and tomorrow
are the trinkets of prophets
and pacifiers of historians.

The true toy
does not exist in time.
The Treasure defies its thieves.
As soon as they look at it
it disappears.

Now is only now
not then
not yet
don't chase it
you will never catch it.

Sing a lullaby
to your baby.
Let your mother rock you
in her infinite love.
no fussing
only warm sleep and sweet dreams
opening your eyes occasionally
just to make sure
she is still there.

SADNESS OF GUITARS

for Jason

Why do I practice anger
when it is peace that I want?

What if something you love
becomes the source of a nightmare
as cruel as the death of a child?

What if your guitars
could no longer be touched
by the one who loved them the most?

What if not even True Love
could move
fingers or hand any more?

The guitars
are in protest
Taking a vow of silence

Because their tongues
were the fingers of my Son
now paralyzed
cut out
by fate's blind executioner.

What if you still love
someone who hates you?

or the music in your head
keeps singing and singing
to no one
but your self
and it makes you lonely?

What if God hears it
and She is moved to tears
but cannot tell you
because that is the law He made
for this angry dimension for learning
compassion
and since She is honest
He won't break the law
even for you?

Maybe She gave you a jewel
in your heart
but what should you do with these songs?
that no guitar can sing
until your resurrection?

MY GUITARS WAIT FOR ME

I have a room
full of guitars.

My fingers are involved in intimacy
with each one of them.

With their beautiful bodies
resting in their own special chairs
my guitar flowers wait for me.

While they are not being touched
they hum the songs
I have played many times on their strings
sensuously vibrating
their fine polished wood.

They wait for me in the light of the sun.
In the warm romantic light of spring's morning.
In noon's lazy erotic heat.
In the clarity of starlight they wait
By the full moon awareness
entering at night through bamboo blinds
uninvited and welcome.
And during the wet
glowing percussion of rain
pounding its gray drizzly drum
Drops dripping from eaves
where young birds were raised
in the down fluff of twigs.

They wait for me in sadness
hoping I will let them soothe me
with the sweet sorrow
of their vibrating sympathy.

My guitars wait patiently
for me to finish my coffee
and kiss the sweet face of my wife.
They want me to hold them
while I think of the curves of her body
and the depth of her heart.
They want me to pour
my cream of emotions
from imagination's silent pitcher
into the cups of my fingertips
to be sipped by the lips of their strings
who want only to joyously vibrate
with real human feeling.

Together
my guitars and I
comfort the lonely silence of space
with grateful melodic caresses of music
Like song birds sweeten the quiet
dawn with their haunting recitals
profoundly awakening
this dangerous mystery's deep beauty
within us.

STREETS

CRAYON MANIFESTO

One by one
you lost every toy
you ever had.

Then
you went to work
with a shovel
or a brief case in your hand.
Still, you are only a few yards
from the playground.

the stars are not even aware of you yet
though you scattered
a trail of self-rising bread crumbs
along the winding path
away from the wide-eyed humility of
your cradle.
Your pride at being a grown-up
is a mask worn by an innocent child
who is always with you
seen but not heard
hoping you will come home again
wanting you to come out and play.

Some day
your marbles and your jacks
will mean more to you
than all your awards.
Pick out your crayons now.
Color yourself a wish.

Learn the magic names:

Red
Yellow
Blue
Green
Orange
Purple

DOWNTOWN RICHMOND, THE 50's

a little drizzle
sprinkling down on the streets
sidewalks shiny
with rain
in front of Kress'
five and dime.

thursday afternoon
a matinee movie
Peter Pan
not too many people out

A mysterious decoration
of tiny tile squares on the ground
slopes up to the doors of Kress'
to its wooden floor.
Popcorn is brewing
in a glass aquarium
with no fish.
Puffy kernels piled
onto snowy corn hills.
The aroma of popcorn
steam heats
the department store atmosphere
arousing an incense of reverence
in toy seekers
and young hearts of all ages.

The toys are displayed in flat bins
like produce in a grocery store.
My mom prefers apples.
I'm partial to rubber dinosaurs.
She sails off somewhere far away
into Bermuda triangles
of kitchen ware and clothes.

I stay anchored to the toys
looking and touching
wishing I could take home
the ones that I like the most
to add to the things I call mine.
To launch rocket ships on my desk.
Conceal secret decoders in my drawers.
Scatter puzzles of winding roads
to distant mountains on the floor.
Station tin soldiers under the bed.
Crash balsa wood gliders
splintering wings out in the yard.
I want the animals of the jungle
roaming the wild areas in my sheets.
I want a King's ransom of marbles.
I want cowboys and Indians.
I need heroes and villains
and books of their tales.
I want fences and farms and tractors
and forts and guitars.
I want galleons and swords
quill pens and parchment scrolls
for weather beaten poetry
of things I did yesterday
and some paper clips and erasers
and a baseball with laces
a wooden top with metal axis
a rubber man with a parachute
little red rolls of paper caps
with small bumps of gun powder
for snapping the air

I want castles
but I don't want dolls
especially the kind with long sexy legs
and removable clothes.
I don't want any white wheels
rolling a carriage

with a baby peeking out
needing diapers and bonnets
or ruffles and lace.
I don't want purses with buckles
stuffed with pink combs
plastic lipstick
golden mirrors
and I don't want bows in my hair
or sparkles on my shoes
no purple irons
or happy teddy bears
no necklaces with hearts
or bracelets with dangling ponies
no little stoves
for me
or tiny pots and pans
in small kitchens for mommies
to make cookies for serious boys
who play with wrenches not ribbons
and there's no need to have a ring
on any of my squirt gun toting fingers.
Maybe some roller skates
with sparking steel wheels
and a box of colored chalk
for drawing maps on the earth
of lost civilizations.

I don't ask for much
just to satisfy
my God-given desire to be happy
and play all the time.

The next block over
past the avenue sign
on the Victorian lamp post
the glittering jewels
of the Theater's neon treasure
sparkle in the mist

in swirls and stars of electric
super nova gateways
to cinema's hallucination
where
Popcorn is Queen
in a carnival palace
of harlequin astronomy
with tiny galaxies of twinkling lights
in a universe of princesses and knights.

be quiet now
the movie is about to start

Peter Pan and Tinkerbell
that's enough romance
for little boys
led by the hand of their mother
over deep red rugs
of Persian
mystical design

it's very dark inside
but it's getting lighter out doors
as the rain lets up

MARBLES

Crystal balls
in the hands of second grade pirates
and kindergarten gladiators
are dropped on the dirt
in a stick-drawn circle.
The beads are quite magical
but they don't foretell the names
of the children who will come
from these masters of glass spheres

Peery
One-eyed Jack
Steely
Yellowjacket
Aggie
Cat's Eye
Calico
Black Beauty

Mystical fetishes of the scruffy
knee-torn shamans of fun.
Precious gems and pirate's gold
were nothing like the legendary treasure
of a leather bag full of marbles
heavy as the weight of cowboy's spurs
willing to be risked for loss or gain
in contests of skill
for school age gamblers with nerve.

In those simpler times
the moon stayed where it belonged
in the eyes of poets and girls,
beyond boot prints of spacemen.

Young wide-eyed suckers
and old seasoned hustlers
mingled on the grass
and dirt casinos of the playground.
Bet your cat eyes
lose 'em all
Lay your best shooter down
draw a crowd.
Watch out for the boy with the slingshot
hanging from his pocket.
Keep your eyes off the girl
with the red pony tail.
Miss the shot and it'll cost you
that black-eyed jewel.
Glass bullet
loaded in the chamber of your fist
knuckles on the earth
one eye closed
take aim.

Those were the days
when nothing was explained.
It was just a big mystery
like the birds and the bees.
Truth was never more than a rumor.
Toy stores were vaults in the Cyclops' domain.
Sunrise and butterflies
were passwords for entry
to important secret meetings of childhood's day.
Sundown and lightning bugs
signaled the Night Monster's opening eye.
Don't listen to your mother's call to come in.
She'll have you in bed
with your marbles in a drawer
gorillas in your closet
alligators on your floor.

1952

Come on in now.
Cartoons are on.

What are cartoons, Mom?
Drawings that move on TV, Son.
What's TV?
It's something like
stick warriors painted on cave walls
with blood and mud
only more violent.

Ok I'll be right there
as soon as this naughty little girl
stops trying to kiss me.

Romancing the clover
Bumble bees hum their busy tunes.
Don't forget. Beware their stingers.

Sidewalks guarded by rubber armies
of shining knights on plastic horses.
Big kids get all the cool stuff.

If I am nice to my brother
I will get a few of
King Arthur's valiant men for myself.

Who are all these kids?
I've been here only a few years
but they seem to have a deep knowledge of
how to play
and not be scared.

Across the highway
the earth rumbles

from rail road yard monsters.
Behemoths of iron on steel
hauling toys and hobos over the land.

Hey! Why isn't that girl
kissing me any more?
Oh
there's a bigger better boy
with more knights than me
telling her to get lost.
I don't have a chance thank God
I am only five.

Where are all the mothers and fathers?
There are more frogs in the garden
than them in the yards.

There's a kitten behind the tire
of a 49 Ford sedan
two door hardtop
power glide transmission
with a cute pink nose
and a meow as sweet as Susie's Q.

I wish I could find
a lot of coins.
I'd get more knights and horses
so the little damsels
who are always in distress
would plead like kittens
"Brave gallant lad, save me!"

Hey you!
Get back to work.
Time is money.
I'm not paying you to dream.

Sir Gary
Can you come out and play?
Yes I can
as soon as this eight hour shift is done
and I shower and shave
and polish my sword.

PLAYLAND, SAN FRANCISCO

Remember
when this was a wind swept beach,
a seagull's hangout
of sand dunes and ice plant,
a cormorants vacation from salt spray
and the biting exhaustion of fishing?
Too long ago for your recall?
Perhaps you remember
when this same seam on the border
of the ocean's great garment of deep royal water
became a magic botanical carpet
beneath an amusement park fantasy
a squawking rookery
of migrating humans dreaming of flight,
soaring above reality's dense gravity?

That enchanting sanctuary of silliness
withered away in a bleak season of neglect.
Something different is now in its place.
Some nothing kind of something
you can't even see if you look right at it
through eyeballs with telescopes or sunglasses.
A towering man-made cliff without curves
and no features or twigs for a nest,
rose from the ashes of nostalgia
an artless geometry
no crystal or emerald would ever include
in its wardrobe of angles and prisms.
Someone you don't even know
lives happily ever after
in that space vacated
by the gear-driven fairy tale of yesterday.

They look out of windows
through a glass of red wine

scanning the horizon for galleons
sailing on dishes of warm food,
watching the ocean pound its emotions
with the breakers of its voice,
this great nautical actor
summoning courage or anger
or infinite bliss
turning the pages of the script
written by Earth's rotation
on a parchment of sand
unfolding a plot of heroic tides.

There aren't many left who remember the park
with its visitors of seagulls and sailors,
or soldiers home from the war
or on their way out,
searching for a girlfriend,
wondering what happened
to the pals from the neighborhood,
eating a hot dog alone by the tilt-a-whirl's
canvas caravan of orbiting tents
laden with a cargo of laughing and screaming.
Proud uniforms starched with brass buttons
ready for bravery
concealing the question
why did this happen to me?
How do you wind up alone
waiting to ship out
while everyone else is laughing
except that old man over there
stiff in his black shoes
and white whiskers no woman would kiss anymore
though she doesn't mind walking
in tight skirts through the mist in his eyes.
Feeding pigeons from his pocket crumbs,
he stares across the chasm of his decades
of surviving his own war
with its bravery and loneliness,

his medals of honor at home with his socks.
Sure, he smiles at the baby in its carriage
pushed along by smart nyloned legs.
But he doesn't get much attention.
A few cigarette butts are scattered at his feet.
A few people feel sorry for him
though he might have invented a marvelous machine.
In the back ground
the haunted ride's black clanking cars
bang into a giant mouth tunnel
with teeth full of screams
of delight and a few stolen kisses
of gold coins on the lips of the young
warmed by the fire of friendship's true understanding.

Maybe you shouldn't be expected
to remember this old style amusement arcade
though its absence is real
and seems like a treasure
you could hold in your hand
and show to the wonder of children.
True, they are scooping up buckets of wet
sand castle memories of their own
at space age super galactic
time traveling warp speed.
They just won't know
of the squeaking old kind made of wood
and bolts of iron and steel
with visible black gears
rotating in hot buttered grease
spinning rides
aflame with cartoon colors
in a living breathing art
with brush strokes
of canvas and grommets and rope
darkness and cork and balloons
bottles and pennies and holes
targets and balls, water and ducks

wiggling ramps and rocking stairs
spinning spiraling floors
catwalks in the rafters
calliopes and clowns
orbiting steel gyroscopic blazing astral dream images
flashing lights and twirling whirlpools of planetary neon
frightening oratory and carnival incantations
sparks from out-of-control rainbow pods
for ramming your friends
and gullible riders
who thought bumper cars were for bumping.
Magic curtains and mystical distortions
of reality's parallel universe
a twilight zone made of tin
the splendor of the jewels of the carousel
rocking up and down to the rhythm of the sea.
The rocking horse stock market rising and falling
outside the ticket booth gate
no one cares about.
The only investment in here is in
giggling and shouting
forgetting and remembering.

If God created a church
you know it would be more like this
because seeking inner peace and joy
was dull work
but a ticket in this place
bought instant release from the past and the future
on a ride in the present
the saints say we always should be in.

Even the cops rode through
on magnificent horses,
their badges and bullets and silver leather harnesses
exposed the valiant knight in the hearts
of these officers looking down from their steeds
to protect us from ourselves

so happiness could sweetly dissolve
in our restless souls
secretly praying in gratitude
like toddlers looking up
at their balloons in amazement.

A breeze would blow in
from shark patrolled islands off shore
with its windy belly
scratched by starfish-sequined tide pools,
spraying perfume from its juniper-combed air
whispering exotic ideas
to people in love
or wishing they were
as they formed into lines
to hot popcorn
cotton candy
caramel apples
humble corn dogs
food of the Gods
paper passes to the glittering rides
holding hands and prizes
watching strangers having fun
dangling their bangles and bobbles.
Babies' balloons tied to little wrists.
The young ones not thinking of growing up.
The old ones pondering the child
they still have in their hearts but their bodies
won't let them out after dark.
The old folks are creepy
the roller coasters dangerous.

Fog
billowing in from the hovering
monster of moisture at the beach
stirring up peanut shells
and ice cream swells
of trolley cars dropping off thrill seekers

and others wanting to be alone in a crowd
to wander about in the space in their minds
with the past as their partner
and strangers for an audience
that won't listen to wisdom
concerning how hard it can be

Because the powerful splash
of the diving bell plunging
into fifty feet of shark infested sea water
has roared up from the depth of the tank
and a labyrinth of mirrors
multiplies crystal reflections of your self
in a maze of confusing directions
with no way of knowing
which one of the infinite
Alice in Wonderlands
really is you
as they stare back from deep hallways
that really aren't there
while a huge plump girl clown
in her glass insanitarium
keeps laughing
and waving her arms
while she smiles
all night and day
with her freckles and braids
cackling with uncontrollable joy
till she runs out of breath
then starts all over again
scaring little kids with her spooky glee
haunting them
until they are old
and she laughs in their dreams.

So step right up
show your ticket
keep it moving

get ready for the thrill of a lifetime
or just walk on past
colorful places to drop coins in
or wait for the secret winds
that blow up the skirts of girls
unveiling the sculpture
of legs ankles and knees
then bounding up stairs for a free fall slide
down a three story polished wood
mountain slope
on burlap bag toboggans
to rubber bumper brakes
at the snowless bottom.

But if you are just too young
and need to escape from these benign nightmares
hold tight to your mother's hand.
Smell the scent of the elephants
drifting up the coast from the zoo
and watch the brave fools climb
to their doom on rickety rails
in careening steel boxes
carving right angles of fear
plunging down
violent steep harrowing
geometrys of speed
up in the sky
where birds lazily dive through the fog
or drop like drips of oil from the sun
to a french fry
way down below
where X
marks the spot of the treasure
buried on the coast
of the good old days.

Shucks.
You thought it would be there
forever
so when you grew up
you didn't care about peeling paint
or rusting iron
or oblivion munching the rocket ride
like a hot dog
because you thought you didn't need it any more.
You closed your eyes
and when you opened them
it was gone.

So who cares?
But then
what about those children and lonely folks?
You know the ones.
They're still living in your mind
wandering aimlessly in your heart.
You ignored them
but they won't ever go away.
And now it's too late.
You remembered too late
that it was here
in places like this
that you wanted to keep
a record of all that you were,
looking forward with a dime in your hand
gazing backward with a crust
of bread for the birds.

Everything changes.
But for the timeless nature of mind
some of it stays exactly the same
hidden in a pocket of your spirit
waiting for a day of awakening
to its importance
for a moment of realization

of its truth
for a glimpse of understanding
of its value
for a warm sensation of gratitude
that you were given a childhood
and it could never
ever
be taken away.

RUBBER ROY ROGERS

There's a stickery old weed
in a vacant lot some where
that concealed my Roy Rogers
toy cowboy
just beyond the reach
of my eyes
making it lay there alone
while time
whittled away
at the stick of my youth.

In the rain
and the wind and the sun
its boots lost their shine
as it merged with the dirt.
Its ambition faded.
It no longer cared to right wrongs
or uphold the law.
It had no more energy
for protecting the weak
from the strong.
Because it was lost
it starred in no movies again.

King of the Cowboys
vanished
on the prairie of playland
existing in a time warp
until it took up a new space
in an old man's sadness
playing in a farewell performance
to an empty theater
for an audience of childhood memories
long gone
ever present.

A LONG TIME AGO BACK HOME

In my childhood's yard
a redwood spire towers
above the black blades of raven's wings.
This giant sequoia
meditating like a tree
ponders the slow passage of time
in its scriptures of weather.
Raised from a seed
half a century ago in my brother's care
dormant in a little clay pot
for eons by the reckoning of boys
finally sprouting a tiny twig trunk.
Its girth now crushes the concrete.

In its shadow
there stands our young apple tree
that struggled in its dirt
suffering the gnawing teeth of puppies
on its baby branches.
This day it is graced
with blossoming gemstones of apple bud jewels.
She's a weathered fortress
but still under siege
by red apple-loving ants on a mission.
Sadly, no girl's initials are carved
on either of these lonely trees.

Before our furniture moved in
the long hardwood floor halls
were dark churches of echo
with small shrines of little toys
left there by previous children.

On the hill down the road
Brahma bulls grazed like great cowgods.

Orion's belt buckle stars strapped to ships
sailing Prussian blue skies.

The yards full of kids
that too soon moved away
from their tricycle home movie episodes.
In rooms lit by television
eating pretzels and candy
they received initiation
into culture's boundless creations.
Then disappeared into regular life.

See how things fall like rocks
into a canyon of deepening past?
Better leave some trace of your existence.
Draw a bison with mud
on the wall of your cave
so someone will know you were here.

ONCE

Upon a time
there was a lunch pail
with a cowboy painted on it.
The tense fingers of a young boy
nervously gripped its rope edged handle
the first day of first grade.
Food and drink were inside it
and an unruly boy kicked the teacher.
We stared in disbelief.
None of us
would ever break the code of obedience
and respect for our elders
seasoned with good old fashioned fear.

On my way home from school
I saw his unhappiness continue
into his dark discomforting house
full of argument.
What happens next is erased
The screen turns blue
then snow

Meanwhile
Mountains were full of white waterfalls
and squirrels needing nuts
from the fingers of boys.
The forest said
this is the home of your heart.

Suddenly I had to go to Sunday School.
A little red neck tie choked me
and I gagged and tried to puke.
I peeked during the prayers
and was nervous about the questions
since I didn't know petunias about

what was his name again?
oh yeah
God.

LITTLE GIRLS

where I come from
girls wore dresses
that hid little panties

if you were patient enough
you could see them
during recess

they knew
we were watching
but they really wanted to spin
so eventually
they would

upside down and around
the metal bars of the playground
the girls finally twirled

up went their legs
down went their dresses
it was over in a flash

boys didn't like girls
then
but there was something about
those panties

ALL YOUR JACKS

Still shining in the grass
after all these years
like a tiny chrome star
pointing north into your future
one of your jacks
right where you dropped it
when Jack chased you
with a toad in his hand
a villain in his head
and a prince in his heart.

You fought him off
with your giggles
scuffing your black and white
shoes on a rock
and wrinkling the fluffy dress
your daughter will not
have to wear
in her tangles with boy critters.

That Jack was so handsome
but such a rascal.
He is your children's
daddy now
bringing home money
to buy little treasures
and a fresh set of jacks.

You were involved
with other jacks too.
Like the Jack of Hearts
and cracker jacks
with all those surprises
too much Ajax
not enough Jack Daniels.

There was jack in the box
another jack ass or two
then a jackal
and it was
hit the road jack.

And don't ever forget
or doubt for a moment
the dream boat
who landed you
hit the
jack pot.

THE SQUIRREL'S SECRET

All my life I kept a sweet nut of joy
hidden in a prickly shell of pessimism.
It's a tough nut to crack
this dense casing of masculinity
around a soft feminine fruit.
Sorrow appears without warning
wrapped in a garland of disillusionment.
Happiness arrives unexpectedly from nowhere
with news of sunlight.

Bad weather is relentless
pouring its rain down all winter and spring.
I'm struggling with these rocks
that shelter wild grasses
thistles and thorns in their tight dirt.
I shovel and cut
through rivulets of rain mud
reclaiming the garden with my body
to satisfy the hunger for peace in my mind.

Baby weeds lodge solidly in stone cradles.
Negativity tucks itself snugly into blankets of thought.
I want both of them gone
but sometimes it seems as though
only an angry energy will do it.
By the sweat of my brow
I yank out disorder
of dandelions and deep bitter roots.
But winters keep coming with clouds
lulling me to hibernate in the warmth of neglect
while invisible seeds
pepper the ground with visions of growth.

Squirrels in the tree
are munching on nuts.

They chew through the shell
to get to the seed.
What's inside is all they care about.
Too often I save the shell
and toss out the nut.
I keep eating from the scrap heap
of serious manhood
so I won't seem too soft
delighting in feminine nourishment.

Sun Moon Wind Rain
whispering in my mind
full of nuts.
If I pay more attention
to the teachings of squirrels
perhaps I sprout sunflowers
and moon blossoms
with benevolent butterflies hovering
above opening buds of generosity
for only a blister or two from the digging.
the squirrels are storing for later enjoyment
the gathered nuts still safely in shells.

My sweet grain of sugar
is firmly embedded in a crystal of ice.
Someday I will crack it loose
and share it with you.

SAN FRANCISCO

an empty hill
with sweet grass
some trees

animals
lots of birds
and bugs

later
a bunch of bricks
and stones
shaped by humans
into cubes
full of cube caves

now hundreds
and thousands
of humans
go into these caves

and cars
and cars and cars
and trucks
and buses and cycles
and Harleys
go around and around
and around these caves

humans go into and out of
and in and out
and in and out
of these cubes

they think they are not bees
but they are bees

and ants
and butterflies
and wolves
and squirrels
and buffalo
and owls

in these very important
cubes
on the empty hill

TOYS

I play
with the toys
in the treasure chest
of my mind.
I reach in
and pull out mountains
and puppies
truth and illusion
sorrow and joy
flowering Guitars
motion and silence
thunder and salt
oratory and raspberries.
When I lift them out,
they are all tangled together
like necklaces.
I can't get a hold of one
without all of them
dangling
dancing with each other.

I separate a few
as best I can
and frame them
to show off what I found.

REAL TREASURE

There is a safe
in our hearts
where we all keep
a Gold Locket.
Inside it
is the heart
of our own magic
hidden there
when we were a child
with the secret promise
to never lose it.

You have yours
with you now.

YOUR REAL NAME

for my wife

Without you
my life has no dream.
My dreams have no life.
Waves leave no patterns of sea shells or salt.
Elephants no longer track
rose petals into our house.
Traces of our story
left softly in sand
get blown to oblivion
by deep lonely breaths.

I get along well with myself
but there's no element of surprise
like the one you offer
with your eyes.

You make me so angry
I don't think I need you.
Then I behold a wonderful charm
in life's little dime store.
I just have to share it
with someone.
With a thrill in my heart
I think only of you.
As I call out your name
I suddenly realize
you are my one true friend.

I thought your name
was the one your parents gave you
but now I truly believe
it really is
God.

FRESH BABIES

for my twin grand daughters
Sarah and Emma

It's a brand new world at last.
The floor swept itself clean
with a sorcerer's broom
the moment your birth cast a spell
of enchantment on a still life
cluttered with unwashed dishes
and a newspaper folded to the business page.
I thought it would keep raining
but you opened your eyes
and your pupils were suns.

All the stale old tricks
instantly
changed to astonishing magic.
Like tiny twin keys
you unlocked the doors I keep closed
hiding my boxes of happiness
stored in an attic of old age
jaded from knowing too much.
That emotion of youthful joy
belongs in Santa's bag
not the mind of a serious adult.

But when you were born
I heard sleigh bells.
The clock in the toy shop
started ticking and tocking.
The wood chisel went looking for wood
with its ideas of wheels and lips.
There won't be gloomy cobwebs anymore
on my hammer and glue
roped to the bench by a spider,
that night watchman of neglect

keeping little wooden heads uncarved
in birch blocks of imagination
waiting to appear with their gullible delight
and tiny honest noses.
Now nothing can stop yarn
from weaving a dance of dolls.

You babies
with your postage stamp
fingers and toes
We can't wait
to stuff your cuteness
full of facts and fairy tales.
You came ready to use
with moving parts and sound effects
guaranteed for life
batteries included.
You tumbled from your package
into this dream
from your cozy higher reality
sliding down the light tunnel
into your mother's arms
knocking over cups of cocoa
and sleeping in marshmallow cribs.

Don't be scared little ones.
We want you.
We need you.
We will change your diapers
but it's you
who will be taking care of us.

We know all about this universe
you just beamed into.
But to make room for our serious silliness
you soon won't remember
the things you know
of the other one you left behind.

You are masters of love already.
Nothing else matters
though you will have to learn that yourself.
In the meantime
we can frost your dreams
with chocolate coated fantasy.
So forget your old world of light.
Here we keep light
wrapped in beautiful darkness
so the candles of your cakes
can shine like stars.

You brought a hidden treasure with you.
We will find it together little babies.
Suck your thumbs now
while we cook your warm future
on the stove of our hearts.

ART

is the soul
at play

human spirit craves
art
like our body
craves food.
feed it.
art nourishes
the soul.

my art
is a geyser
of emotion
about the wonder of life.

I am a magician.
I turn cloth
wood
nails
colored mud
into a dream
you recognize
as if it were your own.
don't ask me
what it means.
you already know.

Art is
like the Sun.
It shines
on the creative spirit
in everyone.

ART IS IT

The great Saints
of humanity
say the world is
ONE
They say that all things arise
from one source:
MIND
and Heart
of
God.

Even the physicists calculate
there is only
ONE and IT
doesn't really exist.

So can I help it
if my tricycle sprouts
a pumpkin
or a hermit crab
finds solace
in my guitar hole?
Who can blame me
if birds feed on rubies
or Cadillacs tower
over Aztec ruins?
I am not responsible
for the souls of animals
reciting the poetry of rain.
This narrow sidewalk of reality
turns up hill
past shops full of dreams
to the edge of illusion
where cobblestones are clouds and
children are jewels.

FLOODED ROAD

A FATHER'S HELL

If the blade of your child's death stabs you
while you walk from no place to nowhere
suddenly you will want to give away
your house and all your things.

You will knock on the doors of religions
you had scorned.
You will beg for forgiveness
for crimes you never committed.
You will look at your reflection
and see a pathetic frightened stranger.

You will no longer remember the tyrants in power
and your unfulfilled dreams.
You will fall on your knees
and curse at the sky.
You will offer yourself to hell
as a sacrifice
for the life of your child.

You will threaten to become Holy
but find your faith a veil of smoke.
You will see clearly in darkness
the illusion of light.

Your screams of heart pain
will rip across eternity
and land in your own ears.
The hollow universe
will be filled with your emptiness.
You will live and be dead.

The small voice of God
whispering in your heart
will not console you.
You will weep in the black palms of your hands
forever.

SECRET FAREWELL TO A SON

I almost wish
we had many unresolved issues
unspoken between us
buried in my soul
so I could tell them to you now
and lighten our hearts.
But there really isn't anything there
you don't know.
When I reach inside my grief
to toss out the hurts
and ego scars
I only find
love and forgiveness.
We have shared that many times.
We know a peaceful heart
gives strength and gratitude.
But it cannot stop the flow of sorrow
pressing against it
like relentless mud
obscuring love
so we keep forgetting it
then in grief remembering.

It is easy to forgive you.
It is hard to forgive myself.
So many people telling you
how to cure your disease.
I combat my aches and pains
with anger
while preaching surrender and peace to you.
When it came time to release my ego
I embraced it instead.
I could not do what I knew was right.

I looked in my heart
and found a gun in the drawer

I pointed it at you
then held it to my head
and threw it out the window.
When I looked
it was in the drawer again.

I am talking like this
not to bring up the past
and humiliate myself.
I just want to say...

I don't know what to say
I just want to say something.
Words are so weak.
It is feelings that have power.
Your pain
is my pain.
You are in my heart.
We are not separate.
Others may know you.
I know you as man
and little boy
and all the stages in between
perhaps before birth
and long after death.

I was a little boy
before you.
We met on a street of toys.
We spoke with sea shells
in a voice of guitars
read by books of fingers.

On a mountain top of love
over looking a canyon of sadness
we are together
in the unknown.

This was told to me
by a voice
in my heart.

NERVE TEST

my son who was an athlete
falls on his face in the driveway
with a disease of the nerves
and he calls to me
that he's all right
because he crashed so loud
he knows I heard it
and am crying running to him
in a panic

yesterday
I watched his fingers
fly like wind
surge like water
burn like fire
on the strings of his guitar
releasing
the hawks and the doves
of his music
over the humble earth

today
I observe him
barely able
to place a peg in a hole
of a test board
at a neuromuscular clinic

my innocent young son
wants to live and play music.
he thinks these doctors
will help him.
he is a world renowned guitarist
playing the strings of its heart

he is a rat
with a number
tattooed to his ear.
under a microscope
he is given a survival chance of
zero
and a projected death of
three to five years

yes, God
enough of his music
and running like a deer.
adios
my son
I love you

GOLD

if there is a priest
or a Pope
or a doctor or saint
or a clown
that can
wave a wand
over my sorrow
and turn it to life
for my son
who is swinging from the rope
of Lou Gehrig's disease

then step forward
out of the dream
you bastard
and do your holy job

are you going to sit on your ass
while an innocent boy
whose crime
was making music
that lifted the heart up out of its tears
turns into skeleton
that can no longer walk
or talk or move
or play or breathe
or eat or swallow
or hope or dream?

do you think that's funny?

why are you blessing bombs
and sanctifying wars?
get out your horns
your tinsels and toys

make a ruckus
with the mumbo jumbo
of your professions
so loud
that God wakes up
from its slumbering bliss
and says
enough of war and disease
play on, my boy
with your heart
more precious than gold

BLACK LIGHT

I am bitter
I am angry
I am frightened
I am empty

my heart
is impaled on a stake
the stake is death
not my own
but my son's

but nothing
is mine

he lives
while disease
gnaws his youth to bare bones

nothing is his
not his body
not his voice
not his breath
not the seasons of music
the storms of his hands
thundered and rained
from the clouds of his mind

not his humor
not his fire
not his dreams

nothing is his
and he is not mine.
if he were
I could keep him

but something is taking him back
and I watch him go
weeping
in my deep emptiness
that is not mine

he watches himself
being returned to the source
and the music
waiting to be born
from his mind
that is not his
goes with him

all that creative joy
was a magic trick
in a hall of mirrors
disguising
the truth
and hiding the sorrow

the deep sorrow
of our parting

the sorrow that is ours
the grief of extinguished love
that is ours

WHY DID MY BABY BEAGLE DIE?

My little puppy
dying from pneumonia
slowly crawls
up my chest to my face
and laying her head on my mouth
curls up to sleep
comforting me
while I cry for her all night.

TRUFFLE

My old dog
waited for me
one last time
in the front seat
of my van

only
this time
she was
dead

Her body
was still warm
but so much heavier
after her spirit
that weighs nothing
left it
a few moments ago.

I lay her on the seat
wrapped in her blanket
with her beautiful face
peacefully pointing to me.

We have one more
place to go.
I'm going to send her away
but she will return
in a small cedar box
to rest forever by my hearth.
I know that her soul
still hovers around
so I talk to her as we ride.
I remind her
what a wonderful puppy

she was
fifteen years ago
when we bought her
instead of truffles
from See's Candy shop.
I don't care
what any stone hearted
existentialist says
about sentimentality.
She gave me more poems
than the Greeks
the Chinese
and the San Francisco beats.

She protected me from
small wooden men
stuck in the ground
barking her little beagle warnings.
She chased balls of croquet
across lawns over-grown
with the laughter she planted.
She looked into my studio window
eager to join me
in the nonsense of art
with her big ears and tiny paws
and her tail of excitement
revealing her joy about life.
She littered the yard
with her toys
and some socks
a few clothes and a shoe.
She barked during rain storms
from inside your coat
because she didn't like
getting her feet or her fur wet.
She told hilarious puppy jokes
like who chewed the velvet blanket?
Not me but I'll do it again.

She could chant silent passages
of comforting dog wisdom
to my broken heart.
She gave me the honor
of holding the stick
she blessed with her growling
and tugging teeth.
She thanked me with
her loving tongue
for the ramps and the beds
and massages for her body
that got too old for her mind
still a meadow-sniffing puppy inside.

One day the warm wind
of her delicate breath
turned to gravel in her throat
so we gave her a final meal
of her favorite fish and a cake
and she died at home
in the lap of our love
peacefully leaving us
weeping
for the loss of our child.

Love can't be measured
or weighed
like gravel or sand
black coal
gold dust or diamonds.
A simple ounce of love
is worth just as much
as a mountain of passion.
I carry the love
of an animal in my heart
unashamed and grateful
for the gift that it is.

PUPPY WISDOM

She was just a puppy
this little creature
who dug her burrow
deep into my heart.

Life is precious and fragile
she told me
and then she disappeared
forever.

PUPPY LOVE

Sobbing and wailing
in disbelief
I buried my puppy
like it was my own child.
As I lowered her tiny body
wrapped in a black silk shroud
down onto the flowers
in the hole I dug
while my heart bled torrents of tears
my grief was deep enough
to hold all the sorrows
of the entire world.

I loved my grief.
It was all I had left
of a silly creature
who gave her heart to me
then took mine with her
into the Earth.

Who was that?
I asked no one
through my tears,
that could
plunder my heart
with a few seconds of love
then burn there forever
like incense on the altar
of my painful emotions.

GOODBYE MY PUPPY

Barely able to drink
a little water
my sick puppy
looks over her shoulder at me
saying goodbye forever
as she crawls weakly into
her tiny bed.